Samuel French Acti

The Rembrandt

by Jessica Dickey

SAMUELFRENCH.COM   SAMUELFRENCH.CO.UK

www.SamuelFrench.com
www.SamuelFrench.co.uk

FOR PRODUCTION ENQUIRIES

UNITED STATES AND CANADA
Info@SamuelFrench.com
1-866-598-8449

UNITED KINGDOM AND EUROPE
Plays@SamuelFrench.co.uk
020-7255-4302

Each title is subject to availability from Samuel French, depending
upon country of performance. Please be aware that *THE REMBRANDT*
may not be licensed by Samuel French in your territory. Professional
and amateur producers should contact the nearest Samuel French
office or licensing partner to verify availability.

be invented, including mechanical, electronic, photocopying, recording, videotaping, or otherwise, without the prior written permission of the publisher. No one shall upload this title(s), or part of this title(s), to any social media websites.

For all enquiries regarding motion picture, television, and other media rights, please contact Samuel French.

MUSIC USE NOTE

Licensees are solely responsible for obtaining formal written permission from copyright owners to use copyrighted music in the performance of this play and are strongly cautioned to do so. If no such permission is obtained by the licensee, then the licensee must use only original music that the licensee owns and controls. Licensees are solely responsible and liable for all music clearances and shall indemnify the copyright owners of the play(s) and their licensing agent, Samuel French, against any costs, expenses, losses and liabilities arising from the use of music by licensees. Please contact the appropriate music licensing authority in your territory for the rights to any incidental music.

IMPORTANT BILLING AND CREDIT REQUIREMENTS

If you have obtained performance rights to this title, please refer to your licensing agreement for important billing and credit requirements.

THE REMBRANDT (formerly *THE GUARD*) was commissioned by Ford's Theatre in Washington, D.C. and premiered at Ford's Theatre as a part of the Women's Voices Festival on September 26, 2015. The performance was directed by Sharon Ott, with sets by James Kronzer, costumes by Laree Lentz, lighting by Rui Rita, and sound design and original music by Rob Milburn and Michael Bodeen. The production stage manager was Brandon Prendergast. The cast was as follows:

HENRY / REMBRANDT	Mitchell Hébert
DODGER / TITUS	Josh Sticklin
MADELINE / HENNY	Kathryn Tkel
JONNY / MARTIN	Tim Getman
SIMON / HOMER	Craig Wallace

THE REMBRANDT was performed at Steppenwolf Theatre Company in Chicago, Illinois on September 7, 2017. The performance was directed by Hallie Gordon, with sets by Regina Garcia, costumes by Jenny Mannis, lighting by Ann G. Wrightson, and sound design and original music by Elisheba Ittoop. Dramaturgical work was provided by Daniel Washelesky. The production stage manager was Laura D. Glenn. The cast was as follows:

HENRY / REMBRANDT	Francis Guinan
DODGER / TITUS	Ty Olwin
MADELINE / HENNY	Karen Rodriguez
JONNY / MARTIN	Gabriel Ruiz
SIMON / HOMER	John Mahoney

CHARACTERS

ACTOR ONE
(male, 50s–60s)

HENRY – museum guard; bookish, grieving but in denial
REMBRANDT – the painter; brilliant, grumpy, soft-hearted

ACTOR TWO
(male, early 20s; plays 13–24)

DODGER – training to be a guard; subversive, tattooed seeker
TITUS – Rembrandt's son; clever, loves his father, pragmatic

ACTOR THREE
(female, early/mid-20s)

MADELINE – art student; forthright, grieving, not afraid to argue
HENNY – Rembrandt's partner; loving, practical, grounded

ACTOR FOUR
(male, 30s–40s)

JONNY – guard; military background, carries a gun, caring in his way
MARTIN – hospice care nurse; strong, knowing

ACTOR FIVE
(male, 60s–70s)

SIMON – Henry's husband; a poet, an inherent grace and toughness
HOMER – the ancient poet; visionary, crude, crazy, brilliant

Please don't make everyone white.

SETTING

A large, spacious room with walls that can change color to reflect:
White – present day, a major art museum in the United States
Red – 1653, a luxurious home in Amsterdam
Ochre – roughly 800 BC, a temple in Greece
Black – present day, the deathbed of a poet

The four sections connect like four paintings curated next to each other.
Distinct, but connected.

WHITE

(A spotlight illuminates a man's face. This is **HENRY**. *His face shines out from the dark.)*

HENRY. One of the greatest painters of our civilization
Rembrandt
preferred only four colors of paint:
black, white, ochre and earth red.
Because these hues best highlight the color of the skin.
For example:
In Rembrandt's *The Man With The Magnifying Glass*...
the clothing is dark ochre and shades of maroon
his hair is brown and black with flecks of light
the space around him is an earthen black.
So that there
floating in the middle of all that darkness
is the pale and luminous specter
of his face.

I love that.
That set against an immense and layered darkness
the human light is most visible.

> *(Fluorescent lights start popping on around him. Morning in a large room in a major American art museum. High ceilings, clean light. The walls are a crisp, linen-white color.* **JONNY** *and* **HENRY** *are opening for the day.)*

Good morning Jonny.

JONNY. *(Startled.)* Fuck me. What're you doin' here in the dark, ya nutball?

HENRY. Have you ever been to Tucson?

JONNY. What?

HENRY. Have you ever been to Tucson?

JONNY. Arizona? No.

HENRY. Me neither. But the indigenous people of Tucson believe that the saguaro cactuses – cacti? – walk at night. Simon wrote a poem about them (in his second book I believe).

JONNY. The what?

HENRY. The saguaro – you know, the tall cactus that grows in the Southwest? – They sort of lean a little – they really do look like people... Simon called them "disciples of the sky."

JONNY. Okay.

HENRY. Anyway I've always thought that it was true here. That at night the paintings come alive, expand somehow. And then when the lights go on in the morning – on the Manet, the Vermeer, the Renoir – it's like there's a secret alive in the room, as if something vital and mysterious is pretending to be asleep, their inner life tucked beneath a frame.

JONNY. Why are you saying this?

HENRY. Because that's what I'm doing here. In the dark. I like to be here when the shift happens.
From "alive" in the dark, to "asleep" in the lights.

> *(Beat.)*

JONNY. You say weird shit in the morning.

> (**HENRY** *goes about prechecks for the morning shift.*)

Anything interesting in prechecks?

HENRY. Not yet.

JONNY. That's too bad. You heard about that umbrella that got left here last month, right? – Had pictures of naked cowboys in it once you opened it up? People are crazy.

> (**HENRY** *keeps doing prechecks.* **JONNY** *just hangs around – clearly likes* **HENRY**, *finds him comforting or something.*)

Supposed to rain.

HENRY. Mmmm.

JONNY. You gonna do the Anna Wintour birthday dinner? You know, in the Asian wing?

HENRY. Uhhhhh I hadn't thought to. Why, should I?

JONNY. Oh yeah man, she's big in the fashion world. Big. I love fashion. The Kardashians? Love that shit.

Hey – so Twyla asked me to invite you to supper for the holiday. If you're free. I think she's gonna do a lamb or something. If you don't already have plans. I know it's still a ways off, but. She told me to invite you... To Easter...

HENRY. Oooh...

JONNY. I hate Easter. The bunny shit? Hate that. Anyway. You have plans? Or –?

HENRY. Uhhh no, no, not yet...

JONNY. Okay. I don't mean to pry. I just know she'll ask. *(À la Twyla.)* "Did you ask if he had plans? People get shy when their partner is dying."

(Maybe he shouldn't have said that.)

You know Twyla, she's always mother-henning everybody. I mean of course Simon is welcome to join, if – you know...

HENRY. That's very kind.

JONNY. ...How is Simon?

HENRY. Uhhhhh. Still Stage Four.

JONNY. Yeah that's a shame. *(Chuckling.)* You know Twyla and I still laugh about that staff holiday party two years ago when Simon kept doing that squirrel voice? – You remember that? – He kept hoppin' around talkin' about NUTS. NUTS NUTS NUTS!

HENRY. Ah yes. My poet husband and his unusual flair for theatrics.

JONNY. It was hilarious! The staff parties always make me feel like such a jackass, the tie and everything, but Twyla likes 'em cuz they're fancy and there's free champagne. Simon got points in my book cuz he asked me about Iraq. Not many people do that...

(A sad pause.)

JONNY. So how's he doing? I mean, how are his spirits?

HENRY. Uhhh it's hard to say. He sleeps a lot. Or so I'm told. By his nurse.

JONNY. That's – yeah that's some real shit. I don't know how you're doing it man.

HENRY. "Doing it"?

JONNY. Yeah, like, how you're keeping your shit together. If Twyla were dying I'd be a fucking MESS. I'm saying you're strong. You gonna take any time off, or...?

HENRY. Well I suppose I'll have to. For the funeral.

JONNY. ...Yeah. But I mean like – don't you wanna be home? With him?

HENRY. I don't think either of us would like that very much.

JONNY. Really? You guys aren't the chicken noodle soup types?

HENRY. I don't know what that means.

JONNY. You know, chicken noodle soup types. Like if one doesn't feel well the other makes them chicken noodle soup. Don't you guys like chicken noodle soup when you're feelin' bad?

HENRY. We do. We just prefer to put it in the microwave and eat it ourselves.

JONNY. Got it, got it. Well listen, you should take some time, buddy. Looking at these walls all day can't be good.

HENRY. I like these walls.

JONNY. Not me man. End of each day I am ready to BAIL.

(Small pause.)

Well, look, if you're in the Leave Me Alone part of it, I get it, but if not you should come to dinner. Seriously. We don't have to talk about it. Or we can.

HENRY. That's very kind of you, but –

JONNY. Well, just, you know, just – give it some thought. Holidays can be tough. Even with the bunny shit.

(MADELINE enters with her easel and paints.)

(Beat.)

Ma'am this section is closed today.

MADELINE. Oh. I mean, they let me in... I'm a copyist? I'm going to be working on the Rembrandt?

JONNY. You sure you got your dates right? They're painting the hall out there for an installation.

MADELINE. I have my approval letter.

(She offers her approval letter, which JONNY checks.)

JONNY. Alright, well. We're gonna have to check your measurements.

MADELINE. *("Measurements"?)* Okay.

HENRY. That's fine. I'll check her Jonny, it's fine. Go ahead and set up miss. I'm almost done here with the prechecks, I'll be with you in just a minute.

MADELINE. Okay. Thank you.

(HENRY continues prechecks. MADELINE sets up her stuff. JONNY has sauntered over her way.)

JONNY. So you're a painter.

MADELINE. *(No interest.)* Ish.

JONNY. Ish?

MADELINE. It's just a class.

JONNY. That's cool.

(Re: the Rembrandt, down front.) You're gonna copy that one there? That's a tough one. The light... His eyeballs...

(He peeks at her canvas, which is blank.)

Got a long way to go.

MADELINE. I haven't started yet.

JONNY. No I know I'm just messin' with ya.

MADELINE. ...Uh-huh.

JONNY. So is that where the hot chicks go nowadays to meet dudes? Painting class?

MADELINE. *(Back the fuck off.)* Actually it's where the hot chicks go to GRIEVE A LOSS.

> *(Beat. **HENRY** looks up from his clipboard.)*

JONNY. *(Getting the message.)* I got you. That's cool. Respect.

> *(Trying to recover, and also probably actually trying to be helpful:)*

Hey Henry, maybe you should take a painting class.

> *(**HENRY** and **MADELINE** make eye contact, recognizing they have something in common.)*

HENRY. *(Gently, taking **MADELINE** in.)* Yes perhaps I should. Thank you Jonny.

> *(**HENRY** turns and almost runs right into **DODGER**. He makes quite a picture with his rad-ass mohawk.)*

Oh my!

DODGER. Is one of you guys Henry?

HENRY. *(Recovering.)* Good morning. Yes. I'm Henry. You must be Bernard.

DODGER. Dodger.

HENRY. Sorry?

DODGER. Dodger. Bernard is my grandfather.

HENRY. – Oh, I thought they said –

DODGER. I go by Dodger.

HENRY. Alright then. Dodger.

It's nice to meet you. Uhhhh. This is Jonny.

JONNY. 'Sup.

HENRY. Welcome to your first day.

DODGER. Thanks.

HENRY. I'll be training you. Come in, come in, let's get you oriented with prechecks and such.

DODGER. How do smoke breaks work?

HENRY. Smoke breaks? – Uhhhh – I believe they work like all the other breaks – every twenty minutes you'll rotate and depending on your section and team size you'll rotate out every hour-forty or so. And of course your lunch, which is forty-five minutes.

JONNY. Just make sure you smoke twenty feet from the building. That's a Thing.

DODGER. Okay.

JONNY. I'm serious. And show this guy some respect. Been here longer than most of the art.

DODGER. What the fuck man?

HENRY. Alright, let's begin shall we?

(Brief standoff, but JONNY decides to let it slide for Henry's sake.)

JONNY. I'll check in with you later buddy – Twyla makes a great lamb...

(Exiting, loudly.) I'll be the good-looking man with a gun. If anyone needs me.

HENRY. *(As JONNY leaves.)* That's very reassuring Jonny thank you.

(Once he's gone.) Sorry about that. Jonny is what we call an SPO – Security Protection Officer. Different unit than us. They carry guns. We're the GPOs – General Protection Officers. I don't know why we can't just be called Museum Guards, it seems simple enough to me, but there you have it.

There are basically three types you'll encounter on staff with you here at the museum – There are the retired military and government agency types. You can tell who they are right away. It can be a little unsettling at first – guns, metal detectors – but you'll get used to it. Most of them mean well and just try to do their job.

Then there are the retired teachers, people who want to do something simple, something that allows them to be around the art and people without too much responsibility. And then of course there are the artists, like yourself. There was even a year when the guards got together and produced a show of their work. It was really interesting, I can tell you.

DODGER. How do you know I'm an artist?

HENRY. *(Surveying the tattoos, the hair.)* Just a hunch. Now, I think first –

DODGER. So which are you?

HENRY. I'm sorry?

DODGER. The three types. Which are you?

HENRY. Oh. I guess I'm an amalgamation. I taught art history in a small boarding school and at one time I fancied myself a painter. Anyway.

So! – Welcome to the museum! It's a quiet morning, which is nice, gives you a chance to get the lay of the land.

> *(**HENRY** plows through the following with quick pace.)*

I assume they showed you our entrance by the loading dock? – You'll use that to enter and exit the museum, we'll make sure you know where your locker is. You leave your uniform here, you know, where it is laundered for you, and then every morning you'll attend the team meeting – they're easy – just covering any events going on in the museum, opportunities for overtime, which you'll find you want since the pay is rather DIRE. So let's walk through the morning procedure.

> *(Throughout all of this **MADELINE** has been seated getting herself ready, preparing her canvas, studying the painting. **DODGER** may occasionally steal a glance over to her.)*

Oh I almost forgot about you! We have a copyist here with us today, you'll see them around the museum from time to time. It's rather lovely – having someone here *painting* reminds our patrons that once upon a time all the paintings they see now *were painted*! An artist sat in front of a blank canvas and tried to communicate a truth from the human condition in the language of composition and color... Lucky for us our job today is simply to make sure their canvas is the proper size.

(*They stand by Madeline's canvas.*)

So, they went through her bag at the door of course, so we'll just do this quickly and leave you to it. It cannot be the same size as the original; so in this case the Rembrandt is 143.5 by 136.5 cm, so less than that. Here you are –

(**HENRY** *produces a little tape measure from his pocket and hands it to* **DODGER**.)

You can do the measurements.

(**DODGER** *awkwardly maneuvers around* **MADELINE**.)

DODGER. Hi.

MADELINE. (*Taking in his whole goth situation.*) Hi.

(*He measures the canvas.*)

HENRY. Alright my lady.
(*With a reverent little bow.*) Bonne chance.

(**HENRY** *hops back to his instruction.*)

So. Prechecks. Just making sure there is nothing new – no tiny scratch or discrepancy of texture on the painting or the frame. If we find anything we are unsure about, we write it on our sheet and report it immediately, and someone from Restoration will come examine the piece. After a little time of doing this every day with the paintings, this intimate encounter at the beginning and end of each shift, you start to realize what a privilege it is.

You'll find your eyes continue to find something new. Something – you didn't see before. And that's an interesting phenomenon, no? – How you can look at a piece a million times and suddenly see... It's mysterious. Because of course the painting is exactly the same, it's *you* that's different.

It's happening even now. Even now you are no longer

the same. You know? Even now – you are changing.

> *(A beat between them. Then* **HENRY** *suddenly whips an Officer's Inspection Report of Objects sheet for the morning prechecks out of his pocket.)*

So! This is the Officer's Inspection Report of Objects! Wheee! Pretty self-explanatory – just fill in the top section, date, gallery number, this is room thirty-nine... Uh-huh right there... Uh-huh. You see they list the different items that might be in the room – paintings and works on paper get tallied together, sculpture, furniture, etc. So first just count and we'll go from there.

DODGER. Okay.

> *(***DODGER*** *counts the items in the room.* **HENRY** *looks at* **MADELINE** *and then at the Rembrandt with a familiar smile.)*

So the bust is a sculpture?

HENRY. Correct.

DODGER. And the sketches?

HENRY. Works on paper, up there with the paintings.

DODGER. Okay. We've got thirteen paintings and works on paper, one sculpture, one piece of furniture (Do I count the bench?) ...

HENRY. No, but you do check the ceiling for any leaks.

DODGER. Okay. Done.

HENRY. You're a natural! Now. Something you'll hear an awful lot about, at team meetings and such, is protection. You see, we're not just here to protect the Art, we are here to protect the Space *Around* the Art.

DODGER. The Space Around the Art.

HENRY. Correct. We have an estimated four million visitors per year, in peak season that's roughly eight to nine thousand visitors per day, and it is our job to ensure that the Art (and the Space Around the Art) is safe. So that is why we rotate every twenty minutes. The idea being that by keeping a shifting façade –

DODGER. Do the guards ever move up?

HENRY. – Sorry?

DODGER. Like, do the museum guards ever rise in the ranks so they can affect policy?

HENRY. What an interesting question. Uhh not that I know of. Though I've only been here since *Ancient Greece*, so perhaps before then. Who knows – maybe you'll be the first!

(Re: the prechecks sheet.) Alright I'm going to run this down to the office. It's your first shift! Don't be nervous – it's a museum. Nothing happens.

> *(**HENRY** leaves. **MADELINE** stands down front facing the audience, looking at a large painting. Her hands are on her heart. She is rapt. **DODGER** stands at his post by the archway. Several moments pass...)*

DODGER. If you want to touch it I won't tell.

> *(Beat.)*

MADELINE. What?

DODGER. You heard me.

> *(She takes a beat, decides mental illness might be at play or that she misheard, goes back to the painting.)*

I'm serious.

> *(She looks at him.)*

You can touch it.
Touch it.
Touch the Art.
I won't tell.

You know you want to.
Go on.
Touch it.
Touch the Art.
Quick.
I can't protect you long.

Go on.

This is your moment.

Touch the Art.

Touch it.

Become part of its history.

Go on.

Touch it.

Touch it.

Touch it.

Touch –

MADELINE. *(Shaming him, very firm.)* Stop. Stop that. I'm not going to touch the Art.

> *(She feels a little bad.)*

Thank you anyway.

> *(Beat. She tries to go back to enjoying the painting. Even puts her hands back on her heart. She almost succeeds, but then:)*

DODGER. I understand.

You don't feel worthy.

It's the Art.

You're in the Space Around the Art.

You're under the spell! –

I get it.

It's cool.

I think you'll regret it.

Later.

In the bathtub.

You'll think Dammit.

I should've touched the Art.

Just saying.

MADELINE. I'm not going to touch the Art. What's wrong with you?

DODGER. What's wrong with me? What's wrong with *you*? That's the question. You get a perfectly good opportunity to touch the Art and you blow it? Do you realize what I'm risking for you? I see you, your hands on your heart, and I think there, there is a person who would appreciate an opportunity to touch the Art. So I take that risk, I make that leap, and you shame me? Shame on *you*, that's what I say.

MADELINE. Are you mentally ill? I'm serious, do you have a diagnosis? Because later tonight "in the bathtub" (whatever THAT MEANS) I will NOT feel bad for not touching the Art, but I WILL feel bad for bawling out a developmentally challenged bipolar who had a bad day with his meds, you know what I'm saying?

DODGER. *(A little cowed.)* My mother was bipolar.

MADELINE. Don't tell people to touch the Art. Are you going to tell people to touch the Art? Don't do that. Are you going to do that?

DODGER. No.

MADELINE. Don't lie to me.

DODGER. I'm not. You just seem like someone who deeply loves Art –

MADELINE. I do, I do deeply love Art.

DODGER. Okay, and I think it would be good to bring Art and people together, not further apart, break down the divide so that people won't feel – so – alienated.

MADELINE. That "divide" as you call it is not there to make people feel alienated it's there to protect the Art from the grimy shit on our fingers, like chicken grease, which yes maybe I just had because maybe I've been feeling a little sad and unmoored lately and I thought fried chicken would help, because I used to have it a lot as a child, which is not the point, the point is that we don't touch the Art because it will HARM the Art, and then NO ONE will be able to become "a part of the Art's history" because the Art will be RUINED.

DODGER. I never thought of it that way.

MADELINE. How did you get this job?

DODGER. Please don't report me. I wanna rise up the chain of command so I can affect change.

MADELINE. Well you're off to a bad start.

(She stares back at the painting, suddenly consumed with the idea of touching it.)

MADELINE. Have you ever touched the Art?

DODGER. No. I haven't, I swear to God, I haven't. I just want to. I just want someone who seems worthy to do it so that I can, I don't know...

MADELINE. And I would be worthy why?

DODGER. I don't know – because you had your hands on your heart and you're so pretty. Please don't report me. I'm not mentally ill.

I'm artistic.

(Beat.)

MADELINE. Alright I'm not going to report you. DON'T do that again. No one should touch the Art, do you understand? Unless they are trained professionals. Okay? Okay?

DODGER. Okay.

MADELINE. Okay.

(Beat.)

And thank you.

(Beat.)

For saying I was pretty.

(Beat.)

DODGER. You're welcome.

*(Long beat. She stares forward, unable to stop thinking about touching the painting. What that would mean. And why that feels so connected to her hands on her heart. **MADELINE** stands lost in thought for a moment, looking down, brow furrowed. **DODGER** watches.)*

Are you okay?

MADELINE. Stop watching me.

DODGER. Sorry.

MADELINE. Don't you have something else to do?

DODGER. No... You look – *peaked.*

MADELINE. Stop watching me.

DODGER. I have to watch you it's my job.

MADELINE. Well stop.

DODGER. Sorry.

MADELINE. *Peaked?*

DODGER. ...Sorry.

> (*She continues to stand there in front of the painting, facing the audience. She seems unable to move – to sit back down and paint – or to cry – or to make a friend – all of which would probably help her.*)

MADELINE. There's nothing wrong with rules.

DODGER. Did you really just say that?

MADELINE. What? There's not.

DODGER. Of course there is.

MADELINE. No there's not.

DODGER. Rules SUCK.

MADELINE. *Rules SUCK?* What, did you like read that on a t-shirt?

DODGER. Don't tell me you think rules are *good?*

MADELINE. Of course I do. Rules tell you how to live, what's wrong with that?

DODGER. Rules don't tell you how to live, *morals* tell you that. And you already know how to live.
You're here communicating with Art. You're ahead of most of the world.

MADELINE. You're the weirdest person I have ever met.

DODGER. Thank you.

MADELINE. It wasn't...a...compl– ...

> (*She gets a wave of lightheadedness.*)

DODGER. Are you okay?

MADELINE. ...No – I need – to just – I'm –

(She sits down right where she is, right in front of the painting down center. **DODGER** *comes to her.)*

DODGER. Okay okay just sit right there. Sit right there. Yeah you look – you're still very pretty but you do look a little – sweaty – like your eyes are watery and your pupils are dilated.

MADELINE. I need to just. Sit. For a moment.

DODGER. Okay. Uh. Do you want me to go get you some water?

MADELINE. No.

(He looks around for a moment. No one is around.)

DODGER. Should I go call someone?

MADELINE. I have some water in my bag.

(He gets it out and hands it to her. She takes a sip. He crouches next to her.)

DODGER. Is that better?

(She nods. A quiet beat. Her eyes are closed.)

MADELINE. Will you just hold my hand? For a moment?

DODGER. ...Sure. Yes.

(He takes her hand. They stay like that for a moment.)

MADELINE. Do you ever feel...like your whole life is ahead of you...and you're not sure...

DODGER. ...You're not sure what?

MADELINE. *(Searching.)* I don't know – you're not sure... *why*.

(They sit for another moment.)

DODGER. What's your name?

MADELINE. Madeline.

DODGER. Madeline. I'm Dodger.

(He gives her hand a little bob up and down.)

Nice to meet you.

(**HENRY** *re-enters.*)

HENRY. Oh dear.

DODGER. Sorry. She got – she felt –

MADELINE. I felt dizzy for a moment – it's nothing really – I can get up now.

DODGER. You sure?

HENRY. No no, just stay here for a moment. Dodger we have to file a report. Forgive me madam I'm going to use this as a Teaching Moment – We can't let her get up and walk around until she's cleared.

MADELINE. No really I'm totally fine now.

DODGER. She seems totally fine now.

HENRY. I'm sorry my lady I have to ask you to rest here for me.

(*To* **DODGER.**) What if she gets up and staggers around and knocks over the sculpture over there? This is the protocol. Go notify Jonny.

(**DODGER** *reluctantly lets go of* **MADELINE**'s *hand. He exits.* **HENRY** *and* **MADELINE** *sit quietly for a moment.*)

Thanks for your patience.

This won't take very long, we'll have you back up to your work in no time.

(*Beat.*)

So how long have you been a painter?

MADELINE. Uhhhhh about a week?

HENRY. Oh. A novice.

MADELINE. Yeah. What's that quote? *If you're sad, the best thing to do is learn something...*? My grandmother and I used to come here when I was little, before her MS got really bad... So I found this painting class. I'm terrible at it, but I like it. It's soothing or something.

HENRY. It was Merlin.

MADELINE. I'm sorry?

HENRY. Merlin said that. T. H. White I believe, *The Once And Future King*: "The best thing for being sad...is to learn something... You may grow old and trembling in your anatomies, you may lie awake at night listening to the disorder of your veins, you may miss your only love –

> *(He pauses as if he just swallowed something that hurts.)*

There is only one thing for it then – to learn."

MADELINE. Yes. While my grandmother was dying I read to her. That passage stayed with me.

HENRY. You must have spent a lot of time with her.

MADELINE. She took care of me. Well, the last few years I took care of her.

HENRY. You're very young to have been a caretaker.

MADELINE. I guess so, but... She was my Person. She died. Just last week actually.

> *(She touches a small ring on her finger.)*

She left me this ring.

> *(**HENRY** takes her in.)*

HENRY. You know, there are three types of people who come to the museum.

The most obvious are the tourists. Kind folk who feel they should see that famous van Gogh or Monet, so they zoom through the rooms to find them, and then look around a bit forlornly before they wander out again into this strange thing we call a city.

Then there are the old white-haired ladies (and their dutiful husbands) who have been coming to the museum for years. You know who I mean – this brave, blessed generation of men and women who go to the theatre, who buy memberships, who understand what it means to participate in the cultural institutions of our country – and who are frankly keeping those institutions alive. And who themselves will soon die, leaving the rest of us to CATCH ON.

And finally there are the Seekers. Souls on the verge of an *Understanding*. They look at each painting, at each sculpture, like it's going to reveal exactly what they need. As if any moment it's going to look back at them and say..."*I know you*"...

(She nods. Something between them. Then she rubs her leg, her brow furrowed.)

Are you alright?

MADELINE. My leg is tingling. This has been happening all week – I keep – having symptoms of MS – I can't tell if they're just – psychosomatic or – I get dizzy, a tingling in my legs...

(She starts to panic a bit, rubbing her leg.)

I need to get up. I need – please I need to move my legs.

HENRY. I'm sorry, I uh –

MADELINE. Please. I can lean on you, I just have to get up right now, my leg needs blood, I need to get up. I need to get up right now.

HENRY. Alright. Alright. Let's...

(He helps her stand. He steadies her as she moves her legs tentatively, getting feeling back into them.)

How is that, is that better?

MADELINE. *(Trying to calm down and/or not bawl.)* A little. Sorry. I don't really know what to do with myself...

*(A beat as **HENRY** figures out how to help/ distract her.)*

HENRY. *(Looking up at the Rembrandt before them.)* It's a wonderful painting you're working on, *Aristotle with a Bust of Homer.*

MADELINE. *(Still recovering a bit.)* Yeah.

HENRY. There are so many rich details that make it unique, don't you think? Like the hands.

MADELINE. What about the hands?

HENRY. Oh have you not noticed? – The hands are different sizes! Look at that front hand – it's abnormally large, while the other hand is quite small.

MADELINE. Wow. I've never noticed that.

HENRY. I don't particularly know what to make of it, but I love it.

MADELINE. *(Appreciatively.)* Huh. And look at that little ring. It just *glows*.

HENRY. Did you choose this painting? For your class?

MADELINE. Yeah. My grandmother was the second type you mentioned – the old ladies who support culture? –

HENRY. Ah yes. God bless her!

MADELINE. Yeah, right? – So it just seemed right to do a classic.

HENRY. Well you picked a good one. Rembrandt was at the height of his powers when he painted it.

It was commissioned by a rich Italian named Ruffo, and all we know is that he requested "a philosopher."

MADELINE. Why did he pick Aristotle?

HENRY. It's debated whether he did! There's some pretty good scholarship out there that asserts it was actually Apelles, the ancient painter. Do you notice anything funny about his clothing?

MADELINE. His clothing... Oh! – It's not historically accurate. He's not dressed like an Ancient Greek or whatever.

HENRY. Yes you're very clever! It's true – Rembrandt put Aristotle (or Apelles) in clothing of his own time. Apparently *historical accuracy* is a relatively modern notion!

MADELINE. I love the way he is touching the head of Homer... As if he's trying to connect to the past, find something he can *hold on to*...

HENRY. Mmmm I like that. And see the way his other hand is touching the chain he wears? That refers to the Golden Chain of Being – from Homer's *The Iliad* – the chain that connects the earth to the heavens. Wonderful poet, Homer.

(Beat.)

How's your leg feeling?

MADELINE. It's better. Thank you.

> *(Suddenly there is a "ding" from* **HENRY***'s pocket. He pulls out his cell phone.)*

HENRY. I'm so sorry.

MADELINE. That's okay –

HENRY. We're not supposed to – but my partner is – *Not Well.*

> *(He reads the text. Doesn't respond.)*

MADELINE. Is everything okay?

HENRY. Hm? Oh, just a grocery request. No one's dead. At least not yet. (Ha ha.)

MADELINE. What's your partner's name?

HENRY. Simon. Simon Noth (speaking of wonderful poets).

MADELINE. Oooh a poet. I'd love to marry a poet. Or at least sleep with one.

HENRY. Oh they're terribly dashing as a breed, aren't they? Shall we walk you a bit? Would that help your leg?

> *(They walk in a loop around the room, her on his arm.)*

MADELINE. You met in school?

HENRY. Oh no, he was fifteen years older than me, although we were in a school (technically). He was giving a reading at the school where I taught, and I was *very* young, mind you, I'd never been in love, and I saw him read his work and he was – lit from within or something – I just wanted to touch him.

MADELINE. An older man. I'd also like to sleep with one of those.

HENRY. *(Re: her long list of people to sleep with.)* My lady you have much work to do!

MADELINE. Yeah, I guess I really do!

HENRY. Oh nonsense you have plenty of time. But I have to tell you, after our first date I thought, *Oh don't love someone so much older. He'll die before you; you'll have to watch him – decay...* But – what can you do? ...

(Small beat.)

HENRY. Sorry I'm being macabre. Yes hang out at poetry readings! Great way to meet a – what do the youth say now? – A "Hottie"! Great way to meet a "Hottie."

MADELINE. My grandmother always said, "Whatever blows your skirt."

HENRY. Oh my!

MADELINE. *(Laughing with him.)* Oh yeah! – And she knew how to blow her skirt, believe me. She said, "Madeline, you'll find most of the time the *braver* choice is the *better* choice." She was deeply cool.

> *(They've arrived back in front of the painting, which she now considers in a new way.* **DODGER** *re-enters with* **JONNY.***)*

JONNY. How are we doing here?

HENRY. Much better it seems.

JONNY. Ma'am are you sure you should be standing?

MADELINE. Yeah. I just felt light-headed.

JONNY. I can call an ambulance for you if you'd like.

MADELINE. No, seriously –

DODGER. Maybe a little orange juice? It's vitamin-D fortified.

MADELINE. – ? – No. No orange juice, I'm really fine.

JONNY. Okay I'm going to get the paperwork for you to sign saying you declined the ambulance.

> *(***JONNY*** *leaves.)*

MADELINE. Jesus.

HENRY. It's the era of lawsuits.

DODGER. *(Gentle, to* **MADELINE.***)* How are you?

MADELINE. Better. Much better.

HENRY. *(Noticing their connection.)* Dodger, what's your station in life?

DODGER. Uhhh. I'm a street artist.

HENRY. What does that mean?

DODGER. Depends on who you ask. If you ask the Establishment I vandalize public buildings.

HENRY. If we ask you –

DODGER. Then I create art right on the very walls of public life. Not separate, but right on the side of your bank. Your train. Your favorite deli.

MADELINE. So, in the Rembrandt, who do you think that is – Aristotle or Apelles?

DODGER. Oh Apelles.

HENRY. Interesting!

MADELINE. Why?

DODGER. Rembrandt was saying artists are the real philosophers. We're the ones really studying and communicating the human condition. Poor sonofabitch.

MADELINE. Rembrandt?

DODGER. Oh yeah. Lost everything. His money, his fame, his family. But here he is.

(A thoughtful pause between all of them.)

MADELINE. What is it about museums? They just make it better somehow.

DODGER. Do you think? I think they make people feel more alone, more separate.

MADELINE. But that's why they make it better. The aloneness is the truth.

DODGER. The aloneness is the truth. Rules tell you how to live. Listen to you!

MADELINE. Listen to *me*? Listen to *you*! Museums make people feel more separate? You're a MUSEUM GUARD. You WORK in a MUSEUM!

DODGER. It's my first day.

MADELINE. Somehow I'm sensing it's not gonna work out.

DODGER. Not with *that* attitude it's not.

MADELINE. *Not with that attitude?* You are so annoying.

DODGER. Thank you.

MADELINE. It's NOT A COMP–

HENRY. Can I say something?

>   *(They had forgotten about* **HENRY.***)*

MADELINE & DODGER. What?

HENRY. You two should go on a date.

>   *(Beat.)*

MADELINE & DODGER. What??

HENRY. A date. You should go on a date.
   Just do it.
   Go on a date.
   You're the same age!
   You're both lovely!
   You seem to – um – ENGAGE one another –
   Go on a date!

>   *(They look at him like he's crazy.)*

   Listen:
   She's grieving.
   He can pull off a mohawk.
   It's a match!

>   *(That makes no sense. Another "ding" from*
>   *his pocket.)*

   Excuse me. Dispatch from the House of Death.

DODGER. House of Death?

HENRY. That's our nickname for our apartment.

>   *(He reads the text. Doesn't respond.)*

MADELINE. Henry's partner is dying.

DODGER. Really?

HENRY. *(Putting his phone away.)* Uhhhhh. Yes.

DODGER. I'm sorry to hear that.

HENRY. Well. I mean we're *all* dying, in one way or another.
   Some of us are just doing it a little faster than others.

>   *(Beat.* **HENRY** *escapes by looking closer at the*
>   *painting.)*

Look at that chain. Did Rembrandt really intend for it to be Homer's Golden Chain of Being? Or did he paint it just because it was fun to paint?? I mean look at the thick, voluptuous paint. It's very bold. It *shimmers*. Makes you just want to...touch it.

(**MADELINE** *and* **DODGER** *make eye contact.*)

MADELINE. Maybe you should.

(*Beat.*)

HENRY. What?

MADELINE. Maybe you should touch it.

(**HENRY** *nods, not sure if he misheard or if mental illness might be at play; he tries to go back to the painting, but then:*)

HENRY. What??

MADELINE. Maybe you should touch the painting.
Maybe you should touch the Golden Chain of Being.

HENRY. *Maybe I should touch the painting?*

MADELINE. Yeah.

HENRY. Have you lost your mind?

MADELINE. Yeah.

DODGER. I'm with her. I think you should touch the painting.

(*Beat.* **HENRY**'s *brain just won't compute.*)

HENRY. What?

DODGER. Touch it.

MADELINE. Touch the painting.

DODGER. Touch it.

MADELINE. Touch the painting.

DODGER. Touch it.

MADELINE. You're worthy.

DODGER. You really are.

MADELINE. You're the most worthy human being in this room.

DODGER. Well.

MADELINE. What?

DODGER. You're worthy too.

MADELINE. No I'm not.

DODGER. Yes you are

MADELINE. I'm really not.

DODGER. You're wrong.

MADELINE. I wanted my grandmother to die. Believe me I'm not worthy.

DODGER. What do you mean?

MADELINE. Like I stood at her bed and I said *Please just go.*

DODGER. Everyone wants their grandmother to die.

MADELINE. What??

DODGER. Grandparents are scary! Right?? Eventually?? Not when you're little, not before you understand that Death is going to devour everything you love. But then you start to understand these things and you watch your grandparent get older and lose their dignity and who wouldn't want that to end? It's a major buzzkill.

MADELINE. You're not helping.

DODGER. *(Back to* **HENRY.***)* You should touch the Art.

MADELINE. You should.

DODGER. And so should you.

> *(Beat.* **HENRY** *looks back at the painting like it's suddenly calling to him. It has never occurred to him that he could touch the art.)*

HENRY. Touch the Art...

> *(Something opens inside him.)*

> *(***JONNY** *re-enters with the forms.)*

JONNY. Okay buckarooneys. Here's a form for you, and a form for y–

> *(He stops, sensing he's interrupting something large.)*

What's goin' on?

(Beat.)

HENRY. *(Still with the painting.)* Grief is
mysterious.
It's – the sunlight.
Or certain street corners.
A sudden sense that you're dreaming.
Like you misplaced something of immense value and
have no idea where.
Or how.
Grief is
a profound sense of failure.
Terrible terrible failure.

MADELINE. *(Recognizing it for herself.)* Failure...

HENRY. It's so hard...to love someone.
Because inevitably it's not going to be enough. Or work.
Eventually they're going to –

*(He makes a gesture that mirrors the golden
chain in the painting.)*

Ascend their own Golden Chain
and there's nothing you can do.
Except hope that you helped them, somehow.
And live with the fact that you couldn't.

(Beat.)

JONNY. Well now I'm depressed.

HENRY. So am I.

...

Which is why I'm going to touch the Art.

(MADELINE gasps!)

JONNY. Wait, what?

HENRY. Jonny we're going to touch the Rembrandt. You
should join us.

JONNY. Are you joking?

HENRY. No.

DODGER. Let's do this.

      (**MADELINE, DODGER,** *and* **HENRY** *prepare.*)

JONNY. Wait guys guys what's goin' on?

MADELINE. How should we do this? Like a three count?

JONNY. What's happening?

HENRY. I love that.

JONNY. Guys GUYS come on, let's just –

HENRY. *(Totally unfazed.)* I say we only touch a specific spot, reduce the impact.

JONNY. Step back.

MADELINE. I'll touch the ring.

JONNY. Come on.

HENRY. I'll touch the chain.

DODGER. Alright. Homer's hair.

      (**JONNY** *suddenly draws his gun.*)

JONNY. GUYS. GUYS. STEP AWAY FROM THE PAINTING.

    (They stop and look at him but don't move. **JONNY** *stands there with his gun, very uncomfortable.)*

Goddammit this is the worst day ever!

I just drew my gun on my friend!

Because he's lost his mind with GRIEF!

And said all this depressing shit that I'm never going to forget.

And now I have to go home and ask Twyla if I've remotely helped her up her Golden Chain.

Fuck me!

MADELINE. *(To* **HENRY.***)* Thank you for saying all that. I feel – better.

JONNY. This is really awkward right now.

Henry we've been friends a long time – don't make me tackle you.

HENRY. I'm sorry Jonny.

MADELINE. You only live once, right?

DODGER. We do realize this won't change anything. We're still going to be...whatever we are.

JONNY. Guys.

MADELINE. But maybe not. Maybe something – will *get in*.

HENRY. Let's do this.

DODGER. *(In response to "something will get in.")* What?

HENRY. One.

DODGER. What will get in?

JONNY. Guys!

HENRY. Two.

MADELINE. *(Twinkling with the mystery, the potential.)* I don't know.

HENRY. Three.

> (**HENRY, MADELINE,** *and* **DODGER** *reach out to touch the art.)*
>
> *(Blackout.)*

RED

(Lights up to reveal a large, spacious room in a luxurious home in Amsterdam. The year is 1653. The Rembrandt paintings that were on the wall in the museum are now resting on the ground, covered in sheets. The walls are now a deep red. The bust of Homer is still in the corner.)

(REMBRANDT VAN RIJN *is getting ready to paint. He has had too much wine. He holds a letter from Ruffo, his patron.)*

REMBRANDT. *(Reading letter.)* A *philosopher*? Oh he's got to be joking.

(As Ruffo.) Dear Rembrandt – Paint me a *philosopher*.

(As himself.) Dear Ruffo – No.

(Mutters.) Jackass.

And then he'll write me back –

(As Ruffo.) Dear Rembrandt – Why not?

(As himself.) And I'll say, Dear Ruffo – Because you're a greasy-headed PUTZ.

A *philosopher* is someone who appreciates the dark edges of humanity.

And *you* sir, make BISCUITS. You're a BISCUIT GUY. What kind of asshole has a family fortune in BISCUITS?

And he'll say –

(As Ruffo.) Me.

(An impotent Ruffo laugh.) Hehe hehe hehe.

(As himself.) I bet that's how he laughs: *Hehe hehe hehe.*

(As Ruffo.) Dear Rembrandt – I am paying you five hundred florins to paint me a *philosopher*.

(As himself.) Dear Ruffo – I don't give a pigeon's pecker. *Hehe hehe hehe!*

> *(Suddenly passionate, furious.)*

A *philosopher*

investigates their own face
over and over again,
searching for the bare, miserable, elemental TRUTH.
A *philosopher*
reveals not what you WANT,
but what you ARE.
You wouldn't know a *PHILOSOPHER*
if he SHAT on your FACE!

Actually don't mind if I do.

> (**REMBRANDT** *plops the canvas on the floor
> and squats to take a shit.* **HENNY** *enters on*
> **REMBRANDT** *mid-squat. She's brought bread.*)

HENNY. *(Unfazed, also unamused.)* What are you doing?

> *(Beat.)*

REMBRANDT. *(Caught.)* Prepping the canvas.

HENNY. Is this a new technique?

REMBRANDT. *(Still squatting.)* Yes.

HENNY. And who might this new technique be for?

REMBRANDT. Antonio Ruffo. The Biscuit Guy.

HENNY. Sounds benign.

REMBRANDT. Don't be fooled. Putzes like him will destroy
us all.

HENNY. He's employing *you*, so he can't be that bad.

REMBRANDT. Well.

HENNY. What does he want, this putz?

REMBRANDT. A *philosopher*.

HENNY. Not bad.

REMBRANDT. *(Loud fart sound.)* Pfffffff

> *(Beat.)*

HENNY. My love.

REMBRANDT. What?

HENNY. Get up.

> *(Beat.)*

REMBRANDT. I can't

    (Beat.)

HENNY. Why not?

    (Beat.)

REMBRANDT. I'm stuck.

    (She goes to him.)

I hate getting old!

HENNY. You're not getting old.

REMBRANDT. Yes I am that's why they hate me.

HENNY. Who?

REMBRANDT. The annals of my fickle public.

HENNY. *(Restoring his pants.)* Annals? Don't say annals my love. Your public loves you.

REMBRANDT. But eventually they WON'T love me and I'll be bankrupt and destitute, with little gray patches on my sleeves, the cries of my dead children clanging in my head like hungry coins in in in tiny metal cups.

    (Both are struck with the sudden darkness of this image.)

HENNY. Why do you drink in the morning my love?

REMBRANDT. (I know.)

HENNY. It makes you so maudlin.

REMBRANDT. I knoooooooowwwwww.

HENNY. When I hear you doing voices in here I know you need some bread.

REMBRANDT. *(Taking her hand.)* And so you brought some.

HENNY. And so I brought some. Shall I sit for you?

REMBRANDT. I'm not painting a woman.

HENNY. *(Starting to undo her blouse.)* That's never mattered before. You need company.

REMBRANDT. No no let me work. There's a certain Italian putz that needs a painting. I hate him.

HENNY. You don't.

REMBRANDT. I do.

HENNY. You hate needing him. It's not the same thing.

REMBRANDT. Yes it is.

HENNY. Do you have an idea?

REMBRANDT. Oh whatever – it's always me in the end. It's like a curse. With the lace, the fur, I can get away, crack into something *beautiful* – and then I get to the face and there I am – mucous-y eyes, thirsty lips, worried brow. Me. Every time. And eventually they'll see it. The *Fashion* will see it and I'll be ruined.

> (**HENNY** *has been listening, like a good friend.*)
>
> (*She perhaps has also been tidying, like a good partner.*)

HENNY. How much is the commission?

REMBRANDT. Five hundred florins.

HENNY. Very good.

REMBRANDT. Says you.

HENNY. Yes says me. Says the *annal* of your fickle *pubic*.

REMBRANDT. (*An old joke between them, laughing like this.*) Oh Ha Ha Ha Ha Ha.

HENNY. Ha Ha Ha Ha Ha.

REMBRANDT. (*She made him laugh.*) You're charming

HENNY. And you're grumpy

REMBRANDT. Well bring your annal over here and improve my mood.

HENNY. I'll do no such thing, leave my annal out of it. Eat your bread. I checked your pigment last night – you're fine on red and ochre, but you needed charcoal, so I sent Titus.

REMBRANT. Well we know how Titus loves a good *errand*.

HENNY. Be nice to poor Titus, he's had a very bad morning.

REMBRANDT. And why's that?

HENNY. A package arrived.

REMBRANDT. So what?

HENNY. So you promised Titus no more packages for a while.

REMBRANDT. Oh god. That's a present for you, you know.

HENNY. I don't need any presents.

REMBRANDT. Don't say that, I love giving you presents.

HENNY. My love the very fact that I will never again be someone's maid is all the present I shall ever need.

REMBRANDT. Did you hate being my maid?

HENNY. Well obviously being *your* maid had its perks, but I'd been many many maids before I was yours and yes I hated it. You saved me.

REMBRANDT. *(Dead serious.)* No no. It was you who saved me.

> *(She touches his face.)*

HENNY. Nothing will save you from Titus so you'd better eat some bread. I'll have tea for you in a little while when you hit your slump.

REMBRANDT. My slump. What slump?

HENNY. You know, when you come into the kitchen and pick things up and put them down.

REMBRANDT. What??

HENNY. Every day at about noon. And tea always helps.

REMBRANDT. My Henny. What would I do without you?

HENNY. Stay drunk and run out of pigment. I leave you to it.

> *(She starts to go.)*

REMBRANDT. *(Stopping her, very serious.)* My love. I dreamt it again last night. I was on a dark ship, like some Odysseus. You were naked on the bow, shivering. There was a light on half my face, like here, and I could hear Titus crying in the dark...

HENNY. My love –

REMBRANDT. ...And there was an angry god down in the water... And then you were gone.

HENNY. *(Warning.)* My love stop –

REMBRANDT. Everyone was gone –

HENNY. *(With love, his face in her hands.)* Stop this. There is nothing to be afraid of. There is no dark ship. There is only you. And that canvas. Nothing more.

(Beat. He nods.)

REMBRANDT. A philosopher...

HENNY. *(Holding her breasts.)* Oof I'm going to wake the baby. My breasts are killing me.

REMBRANDT. Good god – the baby! I always forget we have one! What's her name again?

HENNY. Cornelia.

REMBRANDT. Cornelia, lovely that.

HENNY. She's quite enchanting actually. And hopefully hungry.

REMBRANDT. Bring her in here, I want to eat one of her fat legs.

(The sound of the front door.)

HENNY. I will in a bit. I believe your other child just arrived home.

REMBRANDT. *(Back to his canvas.)* Titus? Good, I need the charcoal.

HENNY. Be nice to him. He worries about you.

REMBRANDT. *(Not really listening, working.)* Mm.

(She starts to go, he looks up.)

Henny.

(She stops.)

You're beautiful.

(She smiles. Then leaves. He works. **TITUS** *enters, very pissed.)*

TITUS. You have got to stop.

REMBRANDT. There you are. I need that charcoal.

TITUS. How could you?

REMBRANDT. How could I what?

TITUS. You know what.

REMBRANDT. I don't actually, the charcoal.

TITUS. *(Putting the charcoal on the table.)* How could you buy this damn POT?

>*(**REMBRANDT** continues working.)*

REMBRANDT. Pot what pot?

TITUS. This Asian pot, this pot from Asia.

REMBRANDT. Oh that.

TITUS. *Oh that* he says.

REMBRANDT. That, my dear boy, is a *vase*.

TITUS. A *vase*.

REMBRANDT. An Asian *vase* and a very *elegant* one at that.

TITUS. Elegant? I believe the "e" word you're looking for is "expensive."

REMBRANDT. *(Takes the vase from him, sets it aside.)* Well of course it was *expensive*; beautiful things of quality usually are. I make my living on this principle, lest we forget.

TITUS. It's precisely your living that I'm talking about.

REMBRANDT. Is it? I thought we were talking about a pot.

TITUS. You can't keep spending like this.

REMBRANDT. Like what?

TITUS. Like an emperor or something. You just bought this huge house in the most ridiculous part of town.

REMBRANDT. Which you don't seem to mind living in.

TITUS. Of course I don't mind living in it, it's not the house I take *issue* with –

>*(He has pronounced "issue" with the "ss" sound rather than "sh.")*

REMBRANDT. *"Issue"*? Is that how the youth are saying it nowadays?

TITUS. *(Ignoring him.)* It's the buying of the house and then proceeding to spend as if said house was not purchased!

REMBRANDT. *"Issue"*... It's like putting a moustache on a WIG.

TITUS. You're always complaining about having to hound people to pay you, and yet you spend like you're on salary with the royal crown!

REMBRANDT. Titus you're your mother's son.

TITUS. And a lot of good it did *her*.

(*A stunned beat.*)

I'm sorry. I didn't mean that.

(*A pained silence.*)

I just want you to be more careful.

REMBRANDT. If it were up to you we'd live like monks.

TITUS. That's not true.

REMBRANDT. (*Suddenly furious.*) Yes it is. Titus the monk. Except I don't know what you pray to, Titus, what is your aim?

TITUS. You, you are my aim, you're what I pray to, do you know how that feels? Oh Rembrandt the genius and it's like yes but have you seen our bank book? I'm the child. Not you. It's not fair.

(**REMBRANDT** *studies him.*)

REMBRANDT. You're right, my boy.

TITUS. Oh god.

REMBRANDT. You are, you're quite right.

TITUS. Now you're humoring me.

REMBRANDT. Humoring you?

TITUS. Yes.

REMBRANDT. What's the difference between humoring you and *agreeing* with you?

TITUS. If you *agreed* with me you'd *change*.

REMBRANDT. (*Struck.*) Jesus. I either need to get smarter or hope my family gets dumber.

TITUS. (*Softening slightly.*) Maybe Cornelia will be dumb.

REMBRANDT. You think?

TITUS. I hope. Right now she's the only one I can boss.

REMBRANDT. I know how you feel.

TITUS. *(Still mad but wanting to be close.)* Can I sit on your lap?

REMBRANDT. *(Huh.)* Of course you can.

   *(**TITUS** sits on his father's lap.)*

TITUS. You stink.

REMBRANDT. Well I'm old. Part of the deal.

TITUS. That if you're old you stink?

REMBRANDT. Indeed.

TITUS. But I'm young and I stink.

REMBRANDT. You don't stink.

TITUS. How do you know? You're so old you can't smell.

REMBRANDT. I can too smell.

TITUS. What do I smell like?

REMBRANDT. *(Smelling his wonderful son.)* Like sweat and bad vegetables and hair. It's lovely.

TITUS. Henny says I stink.

REMBRANDT. What does she know?

TITUS. Everything.

REMBRANDT. It's true.

TITUS. Lucky us.

REMBRANDT. *(Chuckling.)* Lucky us.

TITUS. Do people think I'm Henny's son?

REMBRANDT. Why do you ask?

TITUS. Master Thomlin told her to mind her son when we were in the shop. 'Til he realized who we were and then he sucked up because he knew we would buy something.

REMBRANDT. Do you want to be Henny's son?

TITUS. *(With a shrug.)* I like what I am.

REMBRANDT. And what's that?

TITUS. I'm like her helper that she hugs and tells they stink and then lets have warm apples with cinnamon.

REMBRANDT. Ah lovely. She's lovely, our Henny.

TITUS. Am I crushing your leg?

REMBRANDT. A bit.

> (**TITUS** *gets off his lap, sits down next to him.*
> **REMBRANDT** *has a brief coughing fit while he*
> *does.*)

TITUS. *(Softly.)* Do you think about Mother?

REMBRANDT. Saskia? Of course. Every day.

TITUS. What do you think about?

> *(A painful beat.)*

REMBRANDT. Mostly I think about the end... I wasn't very there for her. In the end.

TITUS. Where were you?

REMBRANDT. *(Far away, like a bad dream.)* Anywhere I could be. Anywhere but next to her gaunt, sad face.

> *(They both remember her gaunt, sad face.)*

TITUS. Do you tell Henny you think of her?

REMBRANDT. Of course. Henny knows grief and love aren't mutually exclusive.

TITUS. What do you mean they aren't mutually exclusive?

REMBRANDT. They're opposites that can co-exist.

TITUS. Like that I stink but I'm lovely?

REMBRANDT. That's right. Or like light and dark.

TITUS. Or love and death.

REMBRANDT. Yes. Well done little monk.

> (**TITUS** *has started mixing pigment for his*
> *father. They work together around the table.*
> *Throughout the following,* **REMBRANDT** *begins*
> *to paint.*)

TITUS. *(The bust of Homer.)* Who's that?

REMBRANDT. That's Homer. Great poet. He wrote *The Iliad* and *The Odyssey*.

TITUS. They were poems?

REMBRANDT. More like stories. With speeches. *Lots* of speeches.

TITUS. *(Crinkling his nose at the bust.)* He looks weird. Was he weird?

REMBRANDT. Oh I imagine so. We don't really know. Kind of like now. No one really knows who anyone is.

TITUS. I hate when you talk like this.

REMBRANDT. It's true. We're all just standing in front of one another, perceiving the basic composition, but the real core of it, this human being in front us, is a mystery. Like a good painting.

TITUS. I know you.

REMBRANDT. Oh do you?

TITUS. Yes.

REMBRANDT. What do you know?

TITUS. I know you like bacon.

REMBRANDT. I do.

TITUS. And it gives you diarrhea.

REMBRANDT. It does.

TITUS. I know your cough in the morning sounds like the wheel at the mill getting stuck over and over again… And you hate rich people and you're ticklish under your armpits and your favorite color is blue.

REMBRANDT. How do you know my favorite color is blue?

TITUS. You always want Henny to wear her blue dress.

REMBRANDT. There's a lot of reasons I want Henny to wear that dress.

TITUS. And you never paint with blue.

REMBRANDT. So what?

TITUS. So that's how I know it's your favorite.

REMBRANDT. You think it's my favorite because I *don't* paint with it.

TITUS. Yes.

> *(Beat.)*

REMBRANDT. Does my cough wake you?

TITUS. Yes. I always hear your cough. Even when I'm at school I feel like I know exactly when you're coughing.

(They both think about Titus thinking about his father's cough.)

REMBRANDT. *(Struck, then redirecting.)* You can't paint with blue because it steals the show. These colors keep the person, the human being, focal – put blue on the canvas and suddenly we don't know where to look.

TITUS. Why?

REMBRANDT. Because blue is the color of divinity, the heavens. We don't need to see the heavens; we need to see *each other.*

TITUS. I told you it was your favorite.

REMBRANDT. *(Smiling, quietly satisfied with his wonderful son.)* ...

TITUS. *(Re: the painting.)* Who is this for by the way?

REMBRANDT. This, my dear boy, is for a certain Italian penis. In Italy.

TITUS. That's generally where Italian penises live.

REMBRANDT. And may it stay that way.

TITUS. Is it going to be of Homer?

REMBRANDT. *(That's an idea.)* Homer – huh – I hadn't planned on it.

TITUS. *(Back to Homer.)* He looks so old.

REMBRANDT. He is old.

TITUS. Older than you?

REMBRANDT. Older than all the books you know.

TITUS. Older than the Bible?

REMBRANDT. Older than the Bible. When I was your age my father read him to me.

TITUS. *(À la gruff Harmen, a joke between them.)* Harmen van Rijn.

REMBRANDT. *(Chuckle, à la gruff Harmen.)* Harmen van Rijn. Haven't they started Homer at your school? I'm going to read him with you tonight. And then someday you can read Homer to your son or daughter.

*(**TITUS** approaches the bust of Homer. Pats his head.)*

REMBRANDT. *(A hint of his terrible dream.)* Met a very bad end, poor Homer. No family or friends. Disgraced.

TITUS. Homer.

> (**REMBRANDT** *suddenly sees* **TITUS**' *hand on Homer's head.)*

REMBRANDT. Look at your tiny hand. How strange.

TITUS. It's not tiny.

REMBRANDT. It is. Look at mine.

> *(They compare hands.)*

TITUS. Mine isn't tiny. Yours is just BIG. Your painting should have one of my hands and one of your hands.

REMBRANDT. Why's that?

TITUS. Then we'll be together. In the painting. Can I touch it?

REMBRANDT. The canvas? Sure why not.

> (**TITUS** *goes to the canvas, gently touches his fingertips to it. He stays there touching it for a long time.)*

Titus? What's wrong?

TITUS. *(Still touching it.)* Someday you'll be gone and we'll only have your stupid paintings.

REMBRANDT. That's not true.

TITUS. *(Quietly.)* Yes it is.

REMBRANDT. *(Trying to make a joke.)* You'll have the Asian pot.

(More serious.) You'll have your memories.

TITUS. I don't want memories. If you're not here I can't sit on your lap. Or smell you in the kitchen.

And if you keep buying stupid Asian pots we won't have any money for your cough and you'll die.

> *(Ah. There it is.* **REMBRANDT** *stops working.)*

REMBRANDT. Ah.

> *(Beat.)*

Oh my boy.

> (*A moment of having no idea what to say.
> Gently:*)

I see it the other way.

I won't die someday because I buy the Asian pot.

I buy the Asian pot because someday I will die.

Money is the opposite of beauty.

And beauty is all we have.

TITUS. Well some of us don't care about beauty and would rather have YOU.

REMBRANDT. Alright. Alright Titus. No more Asian pots.

> (*Beat.*)

TITUS. (*Quietly.*) You've said that before.

REMBRANDT. I have not.

TITUS. Yes you have. That's how I know you're humoring me.

> (*A kind of despair comes over* **REMBRANDT**. *He
> puts his hand on* **TITUS**' *smelly head.*)

REMBRANDT. My boy. Your old man is a very flawed creature. You have to forgive him for it.

> (*Beat.*)

Go on now, let me work.

> (**TITUS** *leaves.* **REMBRANDT** *turns back to the
> work at hand.*)

A Philosopher...

> (*Blackout.*)

OCHRE

(From the darkness:)

HOMER. I don't want it written down!

> *(Lights up to reveal the ochre wall of a large temple in Ancient Greece.)*
>
> *(It is sunset.)*
>
> *(The poet **HOMER** is ranting about poetry.)*

I keep saying over and over again –
Don't write the damn thing down!
That'll fuck it all up!
If it's written down someone can sit and read it *by themselves*,
and that's a terrible idea! Terrible!
They won't understand it.
Not unless it's in front of them in image.

> *(He looks up and suddenly sees the audience.)*

Holy shit.

> *(He stands there and adjusts to this new given, this large group looking at him from the dark... And then he decides to roll with it and continue his point.)*

Well why not...
Do you know what I'm saying?
They need to *hear it* – with their neighbor's smelly armpits and their child's hiccups and some stranger's hair twisted up off their neck from the hot sun.
It needs to wash over them in the air – through their ears, around their thoughts...
You need to be able to zone out on the boring bits.
The Iliad is a long goddamn poem!
I should know, I wrote it, and believe me not all of it is COMPELLING –
So let them think about the evening meal
or what it was like to touch their first breast

and they can't do that if it's written down, if it's written down

they have to READ every word,

IT'S A TERRIBLE IDEA.

I may be old and useless but I know a few things about poetry

and it's meant to be HEARD.

(Calming himself, still eyeing the audience warily.)

Alright squirrel slow yourself. Steady. Steady now.

(Chuckles to himself.)

Squirrel.

That's what my wife called me you know.

Livia.

Ooooh she was a POX.

But I adored her by the end.

It takes a long time for people to learn to live together. And some people never do, I've seen that. But if you can get through all the awful stuff, being separate people and all that, domesticity can really work. Once you've done the procreation bit and you can just let yourselves be the siblings you are – siblings with a sordid past, if you will – you can just sleep with whomever you please and enjoy a nice meal together at the end of the day. It's a boon.

I always found it quite interesting actually, who she'd take for lovers.

I remember when she took up with Hyram, the baker.

Oh he's terribly plain, terribly dull, I never would've thought.

But I saw them one day, he was wrapping her bread, *literally*,

and there was something in the way she took it from him, smiling,

that I knew he was wrapping her bread *metaphorically*...

and that fascinated me!

I spent the next few weeks watching him...

It was a bit weird of me, I admit, but I wanted to *know*!

I was *curious*, you see?

I was curious about him, but really I was curious about HER.

Why she liked this plain little baker with his paunch and bald head.

People cross paths at particular moments in their lives and it's a fascinating thing – ten years ago you'd have never dreamt it and then something about the thing they are and the thing you need... I watched the way he worked the dough in his shop, the pale thick yeasty-smelling flesh, and I thought... *(Like he can sense the appeal.)* Huh.

It's such a shame really – that by the time you're able to really see another human being, not as you know them, not as they pertain to you, but just as they are – which of course is an unknowable thing, a mystery – your life is basically over. It's like it's all about to get a lot more interesting, and POOF. You're out.

(Suddenly very earnest, to the audience:)

I want to put my hand on your head.

Lay my images before your brain through the soft furry mess of your hair.

(Trying out a poem, maybe playing a lyre:)

Bring your eyes to mine.

Let's start the climb – up the Chain

link by link –

scene by scene –

'Til we can feel the gods.

'Til we ARE the gods.

(Beat. He makes a face.)

Meh.

I like the idea though.

Climbing the Chain.

A good poem should make you look down and suddenly see yourself
your fragile, freckled hands and toenails.
Your puckered rear.

> *(Maybe he plucks the lyre again, gently, unconsciously.)*

I was by the river the other morning
and there was a large heron in the stream.
Slender, like a reed of light and mist
I watched it glide from one leg to the other for a few minutes –
When suddenly it turned and saw me –
I saw that we could see each other – and I thought
– That –
That – is what it is to be *Alive*!

We have no idea what the other is thinking, what's it's like to be them...
We barely perceive what it is to be *ourselves*!
We are constantly encountering wild animals!
I'm a wild animal called Homer!
This temple belongs to a wild animal called Jove!
And you're a – well I don't know, what are you?? –
See, it's happening even now! ...

> *(He acts this out a bit like he's the heron and the audience is him.)*

You and I are in a great stream, gliding from one leg to another,
we sense another is there,
and so we turn and see...
You know madness isn't so bad.
One day you're ranting about poetry and then you look up and there's a legion of – what? –
Mysterious creatures looking back at you and you think,
Well alright!

Maybe that's what this whole business is about – Art.
It's practice for the Real Thing.
If we can bear to listen to a poem, or a whatever,
we just might stand a chance of seeing another person...

    (Suddenly frustrated or filled with despair:)

Or – I don't know.
I shit in a pot!
Can you believe it?
Shit? In a *pot*? It makes no sense.
But this will never change!
From now 'til eternity man will shit in a pot!
Death will await each of us.
Stop now – think – you're going to die, and you have no
idea *HOW*!
It's a mystery that floats ahead of us all our lives.
How will you die?
Your mouth full of blood, your organs gasping?
Your legs crushed, the infection set in and unstoppable?
A broken heart?
Old age?
Drowning as your child waves to you from shore...?
Or a chicken bone – like a sharp exclamation point
stuck in your pink throat...

I don't mind it really.
Death.
I don't want to *suffer*. I don't want boils on my flesh
or to fall into a ditch and break my leg and die ripped
apart by buzzards.
But the dying itself bit? – I'm good with that.
I try to look at it positively.
There are so many things I'm finally going to get to
FIND OUT.
For example –
What on earth did Livia see in that Hyram?

I'm going to ASK HER.

(I'm also going to make love to her good and proper, rather than the drab routine I did the last two hundred times or so she indulged me.)

I'm going to kiss her more.

Ooooh that'll shock her! – She'll swat my arm and tell me to go jump in the river (that's what she did when I was cheeky, which was always).

I'm going to see the Heavens.

See what's really going on in all that blue up there...

What a god really looks like.

> *(He looks back at the audience. Suddenly struck by a possibility:)*

Or

has that already happened?

Am I here already?

Did you watch me pull myself up,

grasp the final golden link in that long long Chain...

And start raving about poetry

not knowing

that I am Here...?

> *(He steps toward them, palms open, truly humbled.)*

Is this the Heavens?

Are you...

the gods?

> *(He stands there, searching their faces.)*
>
> *(Throughout the scene the sun has been slowly setting, the light getting cooler and darker.)*
>
> *(He slowly, gently drops to his knees, palms up.)*

Did I write anything of value?

Was I anything more than a poor, blind fool?

Did anyone hear any of it and
miss their son,
or plan a delicious evening meal,
or tell their wife they adored her...?
You'll let me know.
Ye gods.
You'll let me know.

     (The sunset completes.)
     (Blackout.)

BLACK

(A dark room in the apartment of an old building. There is not much furniture left in this room, just a hospice bed, maybe a couch, an IV stand, a bed pan. HENRY enters. The hospice nurse, MARTIN, gets up and meets HENRY near the door.)

MARTIN. Shhh.

HENRY. Hi.

MARTIN. He's sleeping.

HENRY. How was he today?

MARTIN. Did you get my texts?

HENRY. Sorry.

MARTIN. Would it hurt you to send a reply?

HENRY. We're not supposed to have our phones. On the job.

MARTIN. Mm-hm.

HENRY. Did he eat?

MARTIN. Some pudding.

HENRY. Chocolate?

MARTIN. Mm-hm.

HENRY. Good.

MARTIN. He wanted pistachio.

HENRY. And?

MARTIN. We're out. Thus my texts.

HENRY. Right. Yes. Sorry.

MARTIN. Mm-hm.

HENRY. His fluids?

MARTIN. Pretty good. His spirits have improved. He told me to suck his dick.

HENRY. ...No.

MARTIN. Oh yes.

HENRY. No!

MARTIN. Suck my dick.

HENRY. He hasn't said that since 1989! – A cop arrested him for holding my hand at a restaurant.

MARTIN. Well he said it today. Suck my dick. Right in that bed.

HENRY. Jesus. Well, I'm sorry.

MARTIN. (*Affectionately.*) Don't be. Simon makes even suck my dick sound like poetry.

HENRY. Amen.

    (*Beat.*)

MARTIN. You should know...

HENRY. Yes?

MARTIN. He's in and out.

HENRY. In and out?

MARTIN. Of consciousness.

HENRY. ...Oh.

MARTIN. He has moments of total lucidity, where he's his old self, and then the next moment he's gone.

HENRY. Okay.

MARTIN. Just so – you know. So you're prepared...

HENRY. I understand.

    (*Beat.*)

MARTIN. Alright I'm off.

HENRY. Thank you Martin.

MARTIN. Sure thing.

HENRY. See you tomorrow.

MARTIN. I'll be here.

HENRY. So will I. All day. From now on.

    (**MARTIN** *stops.*)

MARTIN. (*No judgment, just surprise.*) Really?

HENRY. Yes.

MARTIN. Alright. See you then.

    (*He leaves.* **HENRY** *stays by the door, contemplating the sleeping* **SIMON** *across the room. A beat.*)

SIMON. *(Eyes still closed.)* Fuck you.

HENRY. *(Startled.)* Oh Jesus. You're awake.

SIMON. *(Mocking their exchange.)* The living bonding over the dead.

HENRY. Martin said you were asleep.

SIMON. "Amen." Assholes.

HENRY. You scared me you know; "Fuck you" coming from the dark like a ghost.

SIMON. Oh just you wait. I'm gonna haunt you like the Cask of Amonti-fucking-llado.

HENRY. Simon.

SIMON. *(Making haunting ghost sounds.)* Oooooooooh.

> (**SIMON** coughs. His voice is weak, but he's himself.)

HENRY. Simon stop.

SIMON. You didn't get the pudding.

HENRY. You had chocolate.

SIMON. Chocolate tastes like plastic now.

HENRY. I'll run out first thing in the morning. You'll have pistachio pudding before you can say:
"Suck my dick."

> (**HENRY** gives him a look.)

SIMON. He deserved it.

HENRY. I doubt that very much.

SIMON. He was trying to make me shit in that thing again – that plastic pot – and I told him I was DONE – he said I wasn't dead yet and I still had to behave and shit where people can handle it, so I told him what he could do.

HENRY. Suck your dick.

SIMON. Indeed. I can't believe you didn't bring the pudding. I'm dying you know.

HENRY. I do.

SIMON. No you don't. You don't know I'm dying. You just think I'm smelly and sickly and shitting in a pot.

HENRY. When you've spent thirty-five years failing someone, it doesn't seem right to suddenly turn into Partner of the Year. Right at the End.

SIMON. (Failing someone...)

HENRY. Right at the Home Stretch.

SIMON. What are you talking about?

HENRY. All the times I came home from work and you just wanted to go on a walk together.

SIMON. Well you know how I love to creeper our neighbors.

HENRY. And all the dinners I finished first and left the table to read the paper because you eat so *interminably slow.*

SIMON. (My delicate constitution.)

HENRY. And left you sitting at the table...alone...

(He shakes his head with the pain of that thought.)

Or how I always drank too much at your writing parties and accused you of flirting...or hinted you were a burden or... I could go on and on.

SIMON. Don't be dramatic.

HENRY. I have been vain. And petty. And eremitic.

SIMON. Eremitic? Don't say eremitic.

HENRY. And MEAN. And COWARDLY.

*(Beat. **SIMON** really takes him in.)*

SIMON. Well. I'd forgive it all for some fucking pistachio pudding.

HENRY. Would you now?

SIMON. Yes.

HENRY. Well then.

*(**HENRY** pulls out some pistachio pudding he picked up on the way home. **SIMON** gasps.)*

Ta-da.

SIMON. Add manipulative to that list. And DISHONEST.

HENRY. I shall.

SIMON. And SNEAKY.

HENRY. Done. Shall I also add Forgiven?

SIMON. Get me a spoon you cad.

> (**HENRY** *does.*)

Were you just going to keep that in your fucking pocket?

HENRY. I don't know, I was just trying to find some way to surprise you.

SIMON. (*Chuckling, pleased.*) I should have died while you still had it in your pocket! THAT would've haunted you good and proper.
(*À la tortured Henry.*) "Oh he never knew I had the pudding! I was too EREMITIC."

HENRY. (*An old joke between them, laughing like this.*) Oh Ha Ha Ha Ha Ha.

SIMON. (*Joining in.*) Ha Ha Ha Ha Ha.

> (**HENRY** *sits next to* **SIMON** *while he eats the pistachio pudding. He himself has opened a chocolate.*)

HENRY. I like the chocolate.

SIMON. Well you don't have Stage Four cancer.

HENRY. Neither do you. You're just smelly and sickly and shitting in a pot.

> (*They eat.*)

SIMON. So how was your day at the House For Dead White Men? Did you bring me another umbrella with naked cowboys in it?

HENRY. No.

SIMON. Then get out.

> (**HENRY** *chuckles then pauses, trying to process his day.*)

HENRY. (*Almost vibrating with it.*) I think – I think I had an amazing day.

> (**SIMON** *stops.*)

SIMON. Really? Pray tell.

HENRY. *Pray tell?* Don't become Emily Dickinson.

SIMON. What do you mean *become*? Emily and I have been *ONE* for many years, you know that.

HENRY. *Pray tell.*

SIMON. *(Falsetto, à la Emily Dickinson, an annoying one at that.)*
BECAUSE I COULD NOT STOP FOR DEATH –
HE KINDLY STOPPED FOR ME –
THE CARRIAGE HELD BUT JUST OURSELVES –
AND IMMORTALITY.

HENRY. You sound like a fag.

SIMON. I am a fag.

HENRY. How do you know?

SIMON. You suck my dick.

HENRY. *(Spitting up a little pudding.)* Ha! – Not for many months now.

SIMON. Oh rub it in.

(They eat together for a few moments.)

Lucky Emily.

HENRY. Why do you say that?

SIMON. Here we are, over a century later, quoting her poems.

HENRY. You've published eight books.

SIMON. Well.

HENRY. Well what?

SIMON. Will anyone *read it*? Will anyone quote it while eating pudding with the love of their life?

HENRY. ...They may.

SIMON. Oh shut up.

*(**HENRY** watches him, not wanting to break the spell.)*

HENRY. You're very spry tonight.

SIMON. How do you know? Maybe I'm this spry all day long.

HENRY. You know what I mean. We haven't talked like this in weeks.

Usually when I get home you're out cold.

...I've missed you.

SIMON. Oh god don't.

HENRY. Don't what?

SIMON. Don't start in with some simpering "Don't die" crap.

HENRY. I'm not.

SIMON. Well good.

HENRY. ...But don't.

SIMON. Don't what?

HENRY. Die.

...

Don't die.

SIMON. *(Trying to play the old joke between them.)* Ha Ha Ha Ha Ha.

HENRY. I'm serious.

...

Don't die.

SIMON. Come on.

HENRY. Don't die.

Don't die.

SIMON. Henry.

HENRY. *(Heartbreaking, simple.)* Please.

Don't die.

Please don't die.

Please.

Don't die.

Please don't die.

Don't leave me here without you.

I don't want to be here without you.

My love.

My heart.

Please.

SIMON. *(Taking his hand, a whisper.)* Henry.

...

(Gently but firmly.) Enough.

(He holds **HENRY**'s *hand a moment longer until* **HENRY**'s *recovered, then he pats it.)*

SIMON. So come on. You were Out There today, The World Beyond These Walls – Tell me everything. Any mental illness on display? Did Jonny let you touch his pee-pee in the boys' room?

HENRY. *(Laughing, wiping his tears but recovered.)* Oh you're terrible to Jonny!

SIMON. Well he's ridiculous.

HENRY. He's alright.

SIMON. Of course he's alright (if you drop every aspect of his personality besides the fact that he is kind to you).

HENRY. Well. He invited me to Easter.

SIMON. Oh?

HENRY. With him and Twyla.

*(***SIMON*** experiences a tiny, imperceptible heartbreak.)*

SIMON. ...You should go.

HENRY. Apparently she makes a very good lamb.

SIMON. You should. You should go.

HENRY. Who cares.

SIMON. You need to start doing things without me.

HENRY. Oh shut up.

SIMON. You do.

HENRY. All this was before Jonny drew his gun on me.

SIMON. – What?

HENRY. Jonny drew his gun on me.

SIMON. – Is that a euphemism?

HENRY. No. Jonny drew his gun on me. And I no longer work there. At the House for Dead White Men.

SIMON. ...What are you talking about?

HENRY. I got fired.

SIMON. – You did not.

HENRY. I did.

SIMON. You did not!

HENRY. Yes I did.

SIMON. Don't fuck with me.

HENRY. I'm not. I touched the Rembrandt.

SIMON. Why does everything sound like code?

HENRY. I touched the Rembrandt in room thirty-nine.

Aristotle with a Bust of Homer.

Painted by one of the greatest painters our civilization has ever known.

The subject of which is two of the greatest thinkers our civilization has ever known.

And I touched it!

Specifically the Golden Chain of Being (that Aristotle is wearing) –

> (**HENRY** *holds up his middle and pointer fingers.*)

I touched it.

> (**SIMON** *just sits there, stunned.* **HENRY** *disappears into the memory of it.*)

It was...surprisingly – *spiky.*

The paint.

Slashes of ochre

and black

and white

and red.

I suddenly thought –

Art is such a *slight* thing.

It's a trick.

The closer you get, it recedes, like a shadow.

It *lives*, it *glows*, and then you touch it and it's not really there.

Or it's *ALL* there – Rembrandt. Homer.

I touched *it all*...

Well, specifically *three* of us touched it – myself, this girl Madeline and Dodger.

We counted to three, and we touched it.

SIMON. What the fuck's a Dodger?

HENRY. He's a new guard. Or – well – who knows if they'll keep him on – but they might – give him another chance... I hope so, he's a sweet lad. A sweet lad, god I sound old. I *felt* old, watching them exchange phone numbers, arguing about where to meet for dinner, their faces like wet paint...

(Like it's beautiful.) I felt *ancient*.

SIMON. *(Dreamily, from a faraway place.)* It's as if I'm on a great ship. I'm honestly not sure if I'm dreaming this conversation...

HENRY. I know! I already feel it wasn't real or something... Look at my hand – it looks so LARGE...

> *(The sight of his large hand triggers a memory.)*

I remember my dad reading in the paper that this Rembrandt had been purchased for 2.3 million – and this was 1961 mind you! – And he turned to me, I was all of FIVE, and he said, *(À la gruff dad.)* "Come on Hank, we're going to see what the hell is worth 2.3 million." And he dragged me to the exhibit. We stood in front of it, his brow furrowed, the calluses on his hand... There was something about the way he stood there – staring – as if he felt *separate* – as if it was some Great Thing that would always be just beyond his reach...

I never asked him what he thought of it, the painting.

If he liked it.

If it pleased him.

(I'd like to think it did – that somehow he was – touched by it.)

I regret that actually.

Terribly.

It's just a slight thing – canvas, paint – and yet it contains – what? Worlds. Truths.

(As he speaks, he is also seeing his beautiful Simon, of whom there is only one in all of time.)

I stood there today, and I thought,
there is only *one* of this – in *all of time.*
I touched that fragility
and my heart just...

(Sometime in the last few minutes, **SIMON** *has closed his eyes. He is very still.)*

My love? Are you there?

*(***SIMON*** *doesn't answer. We can hear his breath drawing gently in and out.)*

I want you to know.
You've been
a wonderful
partner.
You have.
I have failed you so terribly.
So terribly.
But I am here now.
I'm here.

*(***HENRY*** *puts his hand on* **SIMON***'s head, just like* Aristotle with a Bust of Homer. *They sit like that for a tender moment.)*

(Then, blackout.)

End of Play